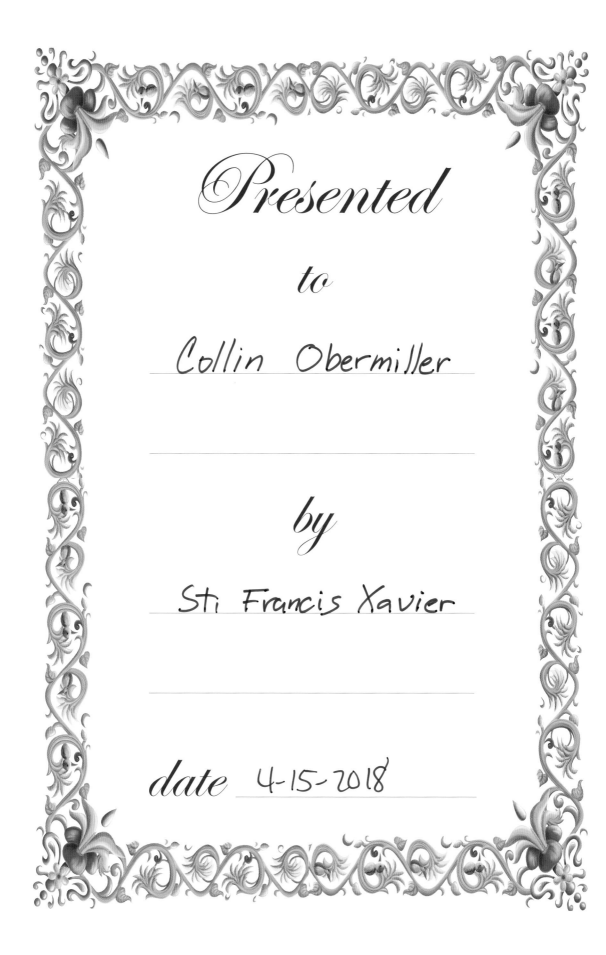

Presented

to

Collin Obermiller

_____

by

Sti Francis Xavier

_____

date 4-15-2018

ST. JOSEPH
ILLUSTRATED
BIBLE

CLASSIC BIBLE STORIES
FOR CHILDREN

●

By Rev. Jude Winkler, OFM Conv.

●

ILLUSTRATED IN FULL COLOR

CATHOLIC BOOK PUBLISHING CORP.
New Jersey

Foreword

God loves us and He wants us to live in His love. But how are we to know how to do that? How does God speak to us and teach us His ways?

This is why we have the Bible. The Bible speaks about what God has done in the world from the beginning of time until the days of Jesus. Even though the things it talks about happened a long time ago, it reminds us that God always wants to be a part of our lives.

We can learn from the very good people who obeyed God. We can follow their example and always try to do what God wants of us. But we also can learn from those who disobeyed God's Commandments. We do not ever want to do what they did.

When we read about how Jesus came into our world, we learn what God really wants of us. God wants us to be His children, and Jesus taught us how to be children of God.

We should say a prayer to the Holy Spirit before we read or listen to the Bible. It is the Holy Spirit Who helped people write the books of the Bible. It is that same Spirit Who helps us so that we can hear God's voice whenever we read the Bible.

—Rev. Jude Winkler, OFM Conv.

Imprimi Potest: Michael Kolodziej, OFM Conv.,
Minister Provincial of St. Anthony of Padua Province (USA)
Nihil Obstat: Rev. Msgr. James M. Cafone, M.A., S.T.D., *Censor Librorum*
Imprimatur: ✠ Most Rev. John J. Myers, J.C.D., D.D., *Archbishop of Newark*

(T-745)

ISBN 978-0-89942-675-4

© 2008 by CATHOLIC BOOK PUBLISHING CORP., New Jersey
Printed in China

www.catholicbookpublishing.com

CPSIA   September 2016   12 11 10 9 8 7 6 5 4 3 2   L/P

Contents

The Old Testament

The New Testament

Introduction to the Old Testament

The Old Testament tells us how God led His people from the beginning of the world until the birth of Jesus. We hear how God created Adam and Eve as the first people in the world. He wanted them to be good, but they sinned. Still, God cared for them.

Over time, people sinned more and more. God punished people by sending a flood, but He saved Noah and his family.

God called Abraham and Sarah to be the parents of a new people, the Chosen People of Israel. God promised them that they would be the parents of many children and grandchildren and that they would inherit the land flowing with milk and honey. God protected His people and saved them from slavery in Egypt during the days of Moses.

God sent kings and prophets to guide His people in His ways. He gave them the Ten Commandments to help them know what was right and what was wrong. He taught them to look at nature and see how beautiful it is and how it reminds us that God is good and loving.

Still, God's people kept turning away from His love. God knew that He had to send someone who could save His people. He would send His only Son, Jesus, to be the Messiah.

The Story of Creation

"In the beginning, God made the heavens and the earth." He said, "Let there be light," and there was light. God called the light "day" and He called the darkness "night." He made the sun to light the day and the moon and the stars to give light at night.

God made the dry land and called it the earth and the waters He called the sea and lakes and rivers.

He created plants like trees and grass and flowers. He then created all of the animals. Some of the animals swam in the sea like

the fish. Others flew in the air like the birds. Still other animals walked on the ground, like deer and rabbits, dogs and cats.

God blessed all of the animals and told them to live in peace. They were to have many babies so that they could spread across the whole earth.

But the most special of all the things God created were the first man and woman. God took some mud and formed the first man and He breathed into him. The first man came to life. He then formed the first woman from that man's rib. God called the first man "Adam" and He called the first woman "Eve."

Genesis 1—2

Adam and Eve

God loved Adam and Eve. He planted a garden for them, the Garden of Eden. He told them that they could eat the fruit from any of the trees that they wanted, except the fruit of the tree that stood in the middle of the garden. That was the Tree of Knowledge of good and evil.

Every evening God would take a walk with them. The garden was a beautiful place, and everything in the garden lived in peace.

But then the devil appeared to Eve, looking like a snake. He told her that she should not obey God. He made her jealous of God, and she listened to his lies. So Eve first took some of the fruit and ate it. Then she gave some to Adam, and he also ate it.

As soon as they ate the fruit, they realized that they had sinned, and they hid from God. They felt very guilty because of what they had done.

God punished Adam and Eve and the snake for the first sin. Adam and Eve would have to leave the garden and wander upon the earth. They lost the peace that they had found in the garden because they had disobeyed God's words to them. But God still loved them and cared for them, even though they did not listen to Him.

Genesis 2—3

The Flood and Noah's Ark

People kept sinning, and this made God very unhappy. He had created people to be good, but now they were not.

Finally, God knew that He had to do something. He would punish all the people on the earth for the bad things they were doing. But He wanted to save one man, Noah, and his family, for he was a very good man.

God told Noah to build a big boat, an ark. Noah obeyed God and he built the ark. All of Noah's neighbors made fun of him, but he just kept building.

When he finished, God had him bring two of every kind of animal on the boat. There were elephants and tigers and camels and all kinds of animals. When they were all on the boat, God sent the rains.

It rained for forty days and forty nights. The waters covered the whole earth, but those on the ark were safe.

When the flood ended and all had gotten off the boat, God made Noah a promise. He told him that He would never flood the whole earth again. He said that the rainbow would be a sign of that promise.   *Genesis 6—9*

The Tower of Babel

FOR a while, people were good again. But then they started to think that they could do whatever they wanted.

Some people built a big city named Babel. They thought that their city was the best place on earth and that they were better than everyone else. To show how important they were, they decided to build a big, big tower. They wanted it to be so high that it would reach right up into heaven. By doing this, they were saying that they thought that they were just as good as God.

God was not happy at all when He saw what the people of Babel were doing. He loved them, but He knew that He could not let them keep on building the tower.

So one day while the people were building the tower, God had everyone begin to speak a different language. They could not understand each other, and everyone was very, very confused. They had to stop their work on the tower, because all the workers did not know what the other workers were saying.

When we use our words in a bad way by lying or disobeying our parents or saying bad words, we are just like the people of Babel. We should use our speech only to help people and say good things about them.

Genesis 11

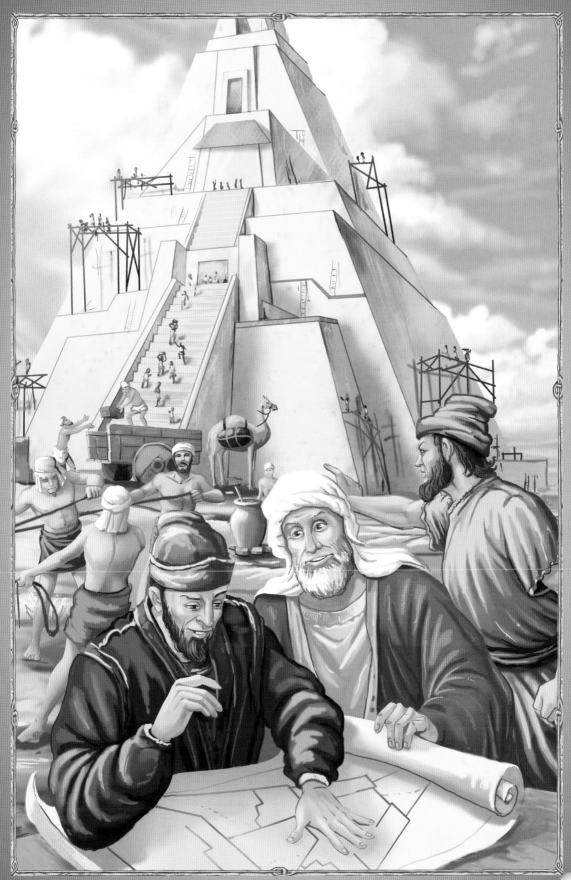

Abraham and Isaac

God called another good man to be the father of His people. He called Abraham and told him to leave his home and go to another land far away that God would show him.

Abraham took Sarah, his wife, and their family and went to the Promised Land. God told Abraham that he and Sarah would have many children and grandchildren, as many as the stars in the sky. He also told them that they would own the Promised Land forever.

But Abraham and Sarah were getting old, and they still did not have any children. One day God visited Abraham and repeated His promise to him that he would have a son. By the same time the next year, Sarah had given birth to a son whom they named Isaac.

Abraham always obeyed God, but God decided to test how much he really trusted Him. God told Abraham to sacrifice his son to Him. Abraham was very sad, but he obeyed God. He took his beloved son up a high mountain and was preparing to sacrifice him to God.

Just before Abraham sacrificed Isaac, God stopped him and told him how pleased He was with him. Abraham had obeyed God even when it was going to cost him the one thing he loved most.

Genesis 12—22

Jacob and His Brother

When Isaac grew up, he married Rebekah and they had two sons. The older son was named Esau and he was a hunter. He was his father's favorite. The younger son was named Jacob and he took care of the sheep. He was his mother's favorite. God had chosen Jacob to do His work even though Esau, his brother, was older.

One day, when Esau was coming in from the fields where he had been hunting, he asked Jacob for some food. He told Jacob that he was so hungry that he was starving.

Jacob had just made a pot of stew. He told his brother that he could have some if he would give up the rewards of being the older brother. Esau agreed, and from then on, it was as if Jacob were the older brother.

That is why, when their father was dying and wanted to give his blessing to his older son, Jacob took the blessing from Esau. Jacob dressed up to look just like his brother in order to trick their father. Since Isaac was very old and could not see very well, he thought that Jacob was really Esau and he gave him Esau's blessing.

Esau was very angry about this, so Jacob had to run away. He went to the land where his grandfather, Abraham, had lived.

Genesis 25, 27

Jacob and His Dream

While Jacob was on the road, he stopped off at a place where people prayed to God. He fell asleep, and while he was dreaming, he saw something very special.

He saw a ladder leading up into heaven. On the ladder were many Angels, and they were going up into heaven and coming back down again.

He also heard a voice that said that He was the God of Abraham and Isaac, and that He would be his God too. God told Jacob that he would have many children whom He would bless.

When Jacob woke up, he thanked God for this promise and he promised that he would be faithful to God. He then went on his way to the land where Abraham had once lived, and he stayed there with his uncle for a long time. *Genesis 28*

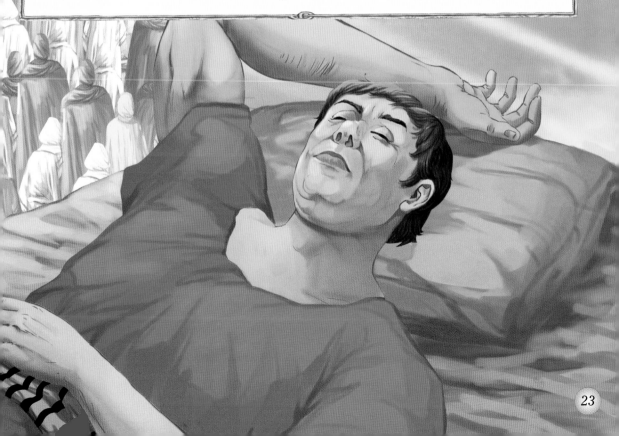

Joseph and His Brothers

God kept His promise to Jacob and he had many children. There were twelve sons, in fact, but Jacob loved one of them more than the others. He loved Joseph.

Jacob gave Joseph a special coat with many different colors. It was beautiful, and all of his brothers were jealous of him.

One day while Joseph was visiting his brothers, they grabbed him and threw him into a dry well. They were talking about what they should do with him when they saw some people on camels passing by. These were men on their way to Egypt, so Joseph's brothers sold him to be a slave in Egypt.

But God loved Joseph and He protected him. Joseph was very talented. He was able to tell people what their dreams meant. He even did this for Pharaoh, the king in Egypt, who made Joseph one of the most important men in the whole land.

Many years later, God stopped the rain from falling upon the land and all the crops died. People from all over the world went to Egypt to buy food because there was plenty there. Joseph's brothers also went down to Egypt.

Even though Joseph's brothers had hurt him, he forgave them and gave them all the food they needed. He and his whole family then made Egypt their home. *Genesis 37—47*

Baby Moses

Many years later, a new Pharaoh who was a bad leader began to rule in Egypt. He forgot how good Joseph had been, and he began to hurt the people of Israel.

Pharaoh disliked the people of Israel so much that he ordered all of their baby boys to be drowned in the Nile River.

There was one boy who was saved, though. His mother put him into a basket and gently placed it in the river. Then the baby's sister watched over him to see what would happen to him.

The daughter of Pharaoh came along to bathe in the river, found the baby, and felt sorry for him. She raised him just as if he were her own son. She called this baby boy "Moses," a name that means that he was "taken out from the water." *Exodus 1—2*

The Burning Bush

When Moses grew up, he found out that he was really from Israel. He started to help his own people, and that made the king of Egypt very angry. Moses had to run away and he ended up in the desert.

One day he saw something very strange there. He was taking care of some sheep when he looked up and saw a bush that was on fire but was not burning.

Moses went over to the bush to see what was happening, and God spoke to him from the bush. He told Moses that He was the God of Abraham, Isaac, and Jacob. Moses was to go back to Egypt and tell the king that the God of Israel said that he had to set His people free.

While they were together, God also told Moses His Name. He said that His Name was "I am."

Exodus 3

Moses Parts the Red Sea

Moses went to Pharaoh to deliver God's message.

But Pharaoh would not listen to him. He told Moses that he would never set the people of Israel free. So God punished the people of Egypt, but still Pharaoh did not change his mind. Finally, God sent an Angel who killed the firstborn of every family in Egypt. But God protected His people from this terrible punishment.

Finally, Pharaoh agreed to set God's people free. He then changed his mind and chased after them with his whole army.

God performed another miracle by having Moses raise his staff over the waters of the Red Sea. The waters split in two, and all the people of Israel passed through the sea on dry land. But when the army of Egypt followed them, God made the waters flow back to where they were before, and they covered the whole army of Egypt.

Exodus 14

Manna in the Desert

God led His people into the desert and cared for them there. But there was not too much food in the desert. The people had brought a little bit of food with them when they left Egypt, but all of that food had run out. So the people went up to Moses and they complained that they were hungry.

Moses spoke to God and told Him everything that the people had said to him, and God sent them a special bread from heaven called manna. Every morning the people of Israel would go out from their camp and they would find the manna on the ground. They would collect enough of it for that day.

They did not have to worry about the next day, because God would give them more the next morning.

Exodus 16

Water from the Rock

But the people got tired of eating only bread, and they went up to Moses and complained once more. They said that they wanted some meat to eat. So God sent a large flock of birds that landed outside of the camp.

The men went out and caught the birds, and the people of Israel were able to cook them for supper. The people had more meat than they had ever eaten before.

Then the people ran out of water. The desert is very dry, and at times it is difficult to find anything to drink. They went up to Moses and complained again that they were dying of thirst.

So Moses prayed to God once more, and God told him what he should do. He told him to go up to a rock and hit the rock with his staff. When he did this, he would get water for the people to drink.

Moses did just what God had told him to do, and as soon as he hit the rock with his staff, a spring of water came rushing out. There was enough water for all of the people to drink. Even though God kept giving His people whatever they needed, they did not thank Him or trust in Him like they should have.

Exodus 16—17

The Ten Commandments

God's people never got lost in the desert, because He led them along the right path. God would go in front of them, looking like a cloud during the day and like a fire during the night, so they always knew where they were supposed to go.

God led His people to a high mountain called Mount Sinai. He had Moses go up the mountain alone. Moses prayed and fasted for forty days on the mountain. At the end of the forty days, God gave Moses a special gift for him and the people he led: the Ten Commandments. This is what they said:

1. I am your only God. You shall not pray to anyone else.
2. You are to honor God's Name.
3. You should keep the Lord's Day holy.
4. You must honor your father and your mother.
5. You shall not kill.
6. You must be faithful to the person you marry.
7. You shall not steal.
8. You must not tell lies about anyone.
9. You should not want things that belong to someone else.
10. You should not want to be someone else's husband or wife.

Exodus 19—20

The Promised Land

Still, God took care of His people. He protected them for the forty years they lived in the desert. After their time there, God led His people into the land flowing with milk and honey.

Moses was very old, and he died just before the people of Israel went into the Promised Land. A man named Joshua, a good and brave man whom God had chosen to take Moses' place as the leader of Israel, led them there.

Carrying the Ark of the Covenant, the priests led the people who entered the Promised Land. The Ark was a special box that contained the Ten Commandments and some manna and the staff of Aaron, the first priest. When the priests walked into the Jordan River with the Ark, the waters dried up so that the people could pass through on dry land.

Joshua 3

The Walls of Jericho

God had promised the people of Israel that He would give them the land flowing with milk and honey. But when they arrived, there were people already living in that land. God once again promised His people that He would take the land away from those people and give it to the people of Israel.

The first city that God's people came to was Jericho. It had very high walls, and it looked as if it would be impossible for the people to take the city.

God had the priests carry the Ark of the Covenant all around the city for six days in a row. While they were carrying the Ark around the city, no one made a sound. The people of Jericho looked down from the walls of the city, but they could not figure out what the people of Israel were doing.

Then, on the seventh day, the priests carried the Ark around the city seven times. On the seventh time around the city, they and the people made as much noise as they could. They shouted out loud and played their trumpets.

God made the walls of the city come crashing down to the ground. The people of Israel then were easily able to take the city of Jericho for themselves.

Joshua 6

Samson, God's Hero

Even though God was very good to His people, they kept sinning and praying to other gods.

God would punish His people by letting their enemies defeat them. When this happened, God's people would realize that they had sinned. They would ask for forgiveness and God would always forgive them.

God would send a hero called a judge to rescue them from their enemies. One of these heroes was Samson. God told Samson that he was never to drink wine, and Samson obeyed this command. God told Samson something else as well: he was never to cut his hair.

Samson was the strongest man who ever lived. Once a lion attacked him, and he was able to kill it with his bare hands.

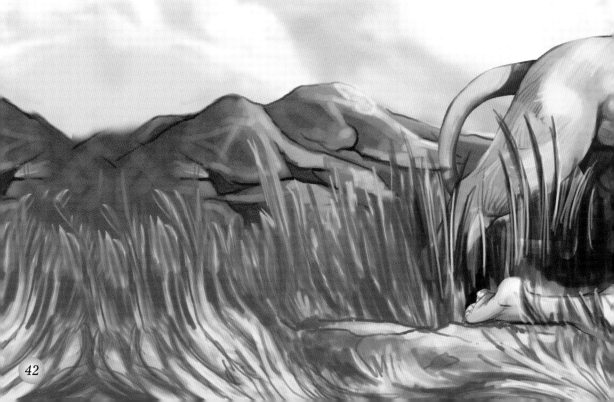

Samson married a woman who was very bad. She found out that he was so strong because he never cut his hair. One night, while he was asleep, she cut his hair. She then turned him over to his enemies who put him in prison.

Later, Samson's enemies brought him out to make fun of him. Samson prayed to be given his strength one more time, and God answered his prayers. Samson made the building where his enemies gathered fall, killing many of them.

Judges 13 — 16

Ruth

Not all heroes of Israel were strong men. One of God's great heroes was a woman named Ruth.

Ruth was not from Israel. She was from a country called Moab. Ruth married a man from Israel, from the town of Bethlehem, who was living in her country. When Ruth's husband died, her mother-in-law, Naomi, wanted her to return to her family, but

Ruth refused. She continued to care for Naomi, saying, "Your people are my people and your God is my God."

Ruth was so good and generous that she traveled to Israel to care for her mother-in-law. She would go out into the fields and gather up grain for their food. God was very pleased with Ruth for she was a truly good person. He rewarded her by giving her a good husband and a son of her own.

The Book of Ruth

Samuel Anoints Saul as King

The last of the judges was Samuel. When he had grown old, the people of Israel went to him and said that they wanted a king. Every other nation on earth had a king, and they wanted to be just like the other nations.

Samuel and God were very sad that the people had said this, for the people of Israel were not like all the other nations. God had chosen them to be His own people, and God was their King. Still, because they wanted an earthly king, God told Samuel to do what they wanted and give them a king.

A young man was passing by Samuel one day, looking for his father's lost donkeys. He knew that Samuel was a judge and that he could see things that other people could not see. He therefore asked Samuel if he could help him find the donkeys. When Samuel saw that this young man, whose name was Saul, was tall and strong, he decided he would be the king of Israel.

Samuel invited him in for supper that night. Then the next morning, he anointed him with holy oil to make him the first king of Israel. From then on, the people of Israel would be led by a king.

1 Samuel 8—10

David and Goliath

While he was king, Saul had a shepherd boy named David comfort him by playing the harp.

When David was still young, the enemies of Israel attacked the land. They had a giant with them, a man named Goliath. He came out of his camp and said that he would fight against anyone in Israel. He made fun of the people of Israel, and even said bad things about the God of Israel.

No one was brave enough to fight against Goliath. Finally, young David went out and killed the giant by hitting him with a rock from his slingshot. Everyone was so surprised that a small boy could do this, but God often uses people who are small and weak to show how powerful He is.   *1 Samuel 16—17*

David Becomes King

God soon saw that Saul did many bad things as king and led the people of Israel into sin. He therefore sent Samuel to choose a new king for Israel.

Samuel went to the town of Bethlehem. God led Samuel to the house of Jesse who lived in that city. Samuel asked to see Jesse's sons, and all of them were tall and handsome and strong. But God had not chosen any of those sons to be the king of Israel.

Finally, they brought in David who had been watching the sheep. God chose David because he was a good and holy boy. God does not look at the outside, but He judges each person by what is in that person's heart. Samuel anointed David to be the second king of Israel.

David was a good king. He defeated many of Israel's enemies. He even took over the city of Jerusalem, where he built his palace. David also brought the Ark of the Covenant into Jerusalem so that the people would come there to pray to God. Jerusalem was going to be a holy city from that time onward.

Even when David sinned, he was humble and he would ask God for forgiveness. God saw that David was truly sorry and He always forgave him. *1 Samuel 16—2 Samuel 12*

King Solomon

When David grew very old, he decided that his son Solomon should be the next king of Israel.

As soon as Solomon became king, he prayed that God would grant him the wisdom he needed to lead the people of Israel. God was very pleased with Solomon's prayer. He told him that if he had asked for money or power or a long life, He would have given Solomon whatever he asked for. But because he asked for wisdom, he would grant him wisdom and all those other things as well.

People would often come to Solomon and ask him to solve their problems because his wisdom was so well known. One day, two women came before Solomon. Each of them had just had a baby, and one of the babies had died. Both of them claimed that the living baby was hers.

How would Solomon figure out who the real mother was? He ordered that the baby be cut in two and half given to each of the mothers. The woman who was lying said that it was a good idea, but the real mother said it would be better to give the baby to the other woman. She only wanted her baby to live.

Her response showed Solomon who the real mother was: the one who wanted the baby to live. *1 Kings 2—3*

Solomon's Temple

Solomon also built many beautiful buildings all over Israel. The most important of these was the Temple that he built in Jerusalem. He used gold and silver and many other wonderful things to build the Temple. He hired the best workers from all around to make it as beautiful as possible.

When it was finished, Solomon brought the Ark of the Covenant into it and he had the Temple blessed. From then on, the Temple would be holy and the people of Israel would pray to God there, even until the days of Jesus.

1 Kings 5—8

55

Isaiah the Prophet

The people of Israel turned away from the Lord again. God sent them another prophet, Isaiah, to call them back to the Lord's ways.

Isaiah first met God while praying in the Temple. He saw smoke rising up from the altar and heard beautiful singing. The song rang out, "Holy, holy, holy is the Lord God of hosts!" At once, Isaiah knew that he was hearing the singing of Angels. From then on, he always wanted to be holy and called upon his people to be holy.

Isaiah spoke of how people should treat each other with kindness and justice. They should not cheat or lie or hurt others in any way.

He also promised that God would give His people a great sign. The virgin would have a Child Who would be called Emmanuel, a name that means, "God is with us." Isaiah spoke of how this Child would be a good King.

He would bring peace to His land. It would be so peaceful that even animals that do not like each other would no longer be afraid of each other. That is what he meant when he said that the wolf would lie down with the lamb.

God fulfilled all of Isaiah's promises when Jesus was born.   *Isaiah 6—11*

Jeremiah the Prophet

A while later, God's people started sinning again. They did not pray to God the way that they were supposed to, and they were not nice to each other. God knew that He had to punish His people for their sins.

God sent a prophet named Jeremiah to tell the people that they were going to be punished. Even though he was very young, God promised that the people would listen to him because he was preaching God's Word.

The people did not always treat Jeremiah well. They blamed him for their problems. They did not realize that they were the problem rather than Jeremiah. He was only telling them the truth, but they did not want to hear it.

They beat up Jeremiah and threw him in prison. Some of the people wanted to kill him, but God protected him and rescued him from their hands.

Even though the people were mean to Jeremiah, he never gave up on them. He told them that God was going to make a new promise to them, a new covenant. This promise would be even better than the last one. In the old one, God had written His Commandments on stone. This time, He would write the new promise upon their hearts.

The Book of the Prophet Jeremiah

Jonah and the Whale

There was one prophet who did not want to do his work: Jonah. God sent Jonah to preach, but he ran away instead.

Jonah got on a boat and hoped to travel far away, so that he would not have to do what God wanted him to do. But God sent a storm that almost sank his ship. When everyone asked why God had sent the storm, Jonah admitted that it was all his fault.

The men on the ship threw Jonah into the water. But before he could drown, a whale came along and swallowed him. Jonah was in the belly of the whale for three days. After three days, the whale spit him out on the shore. Jonah had learned his lesson, and he went to the city where God wanted him to go. There he preached God's Word to all the people. *The Book of Jonah*

The Exile in Babylon

God sent many prophets to the people of Israel, but the people kept sinning more and more.

God knew that He had to punish them for all the bad things that they were doing. Although He really loved them, God knew that they would never change their ways until He taught them a lesson.

So God let Israel's enemies win a war against them. Many people died in that war. When it was over, the king of Babylon, who conquered Israel, took the people from their homeland and brought them to his own country.

The people of Israel were quite sad. They loved their homeland, and they loved praying to God in the Temple. Now, they lived far away from home, and their enemies did not treat them well.

But God sent them some prophets to promise them that their suffering would not last forever. One of these prophets said, "Comfort, be comforted, My people." Their pain was coming to an end.

God promised His people that He would love them and forgive them. He would always love them more than our own mother or father could ever love us. And God promised that one day in the future He would bring them back to their homeland.

Isaiah 40—55

The Writing on the Wall

One of the kings of Babylon was a very bad man. He threw a party at which the people ate and drank much too much. He brought out the holy cups and plates that had been used in the Temple in Jerusalem, thus making fun of God.

But God's hand appeared and wrote three words on the wall. No one could tell what the writing meant until they called in a young man named Daniel. He was a good and holy man, and God helped him to know what He had written.

He told the king that he was going to be punished for his sins. That very night, his enemies would attack and he would lose his throne. And this is just what happened. *Daniel 5*

Daniel in the Lions' Den

Everyone, even the pagan kings, could see how intelligent and holy Daniel was. One king gave him a very important job to do. The only problem was that all of the other people who served the king became very jealous of Daniel. They made a plan to harm him.

They convinced the king to make a new rule that no one in the entire kingdom was to pray to anyone but the king for the next thirty days. Daniel knew that he could pray only to the God of Israel, so he continued to pray to Him, even though this broke the law. Some people saw him praying to his God. They reported what he was doing to the king, knowing he would face punishment.

The king was very sad, for he liked Daniel. Yet, the law was the law, and Daniel had to be punished. He ordered that Daniel be thrown into the lions' den. The animals were hungry and mean, and the king thought that there was no chance that Daniel would survive.

Yet, the next morning when the king went to see what had happened, he saw that Daniel had not been harmed. God had protected him all that night. The king was very happy to see Daniel alive, and he ordered him to be taken out of the lions' den. He then had all of Daniel's enemies thrown in the den instead.

Daniel 6

The Return to Jerusalem

While the people of Israel were in Exile in Babylon, they wondered whether they would ever go back to their homeland. The prophets told them that they would, but it was so hard to trust in this promise. It seemed as if their Exile would never come to an end.

Then, the kingdom of Babylon was defeated by another kingdom, Persia. This is exactly what the prophet Daniel had foretold when he read the writing on the wall. The king of Persia was a good man named Cyrus. Even though he was a pagan, he did what God wanted him to do.

He told the people of Israel that they could go back home again. The people could not believe what they were hearing. They had been living in Babylon for over forty years, and now they would see Jerusalem again.

Cyrus was such a good man that he even sent money with them so that they could rebuild their Temple. He also let the people take up a collection so that the new Temple in Jerusalem would be as beautiful as the old one.

The people set out across the desert. God led His people home again to the land He had promised to Abraham and to all the people of Israel.

Ezra 1

Queen Esther

Not all of the people of Israel went back to their homeland at that time. Some continued to live where they were.

One of the people who lived in Persia was a woman named Esther. Her uncle was an important official in Persia. Esther was beautiful and wise.

The king chose Esther to be his wife and his queen. She did not tell anyone, however, that she was Jewish.

A Persian named Haman decided that he greatly disliked the Jewish people and he especially disliked Esther's uncle. He made a plan to put all of the Jewish people to death on the same day.

Esther's uncle told her about this plot and said that she had to speak to the king in order to save her people. Even though this was dangerous, Esther agreed to do it.

She prayed and fasted, and then she dressed herself as beautifully as she could. She begged the king to save her people. When the king asked who was trying to harm her and her people, she told him that it was Haman.

The king loved Esther and he trusted her. He ordered that the Jewish people were not to be put to death. Instead, he ordered that Haman suffer the punishment he wanted to give to the Jewish people.

The Book of Esther

Bridging the Testaments

Before we turn to the New Testament, let us pause for just a moment and think about the great bridge of the Old and New Testaments: the Psalms.

We read earlier about King David of Israel. It was from his family that Jesus was born. The Holy Spirit helped David to write many of the Psalms or prayers that we still pray in the Church today.

The beauty of the Psalms is that their words are for all times. These prayers speak of thanksgiving for all the wonderful things that God has done. They also tell of the hopes and promises of the Kingdom of God.

Let us give thanks to God from Psalm 100:

> Acclaim the LORD with joy, all the earth;
>   serve the LORD with gladness;
>   enter His presence with songs of joy.
>
> Proclaim that the LORD is God.
>   He made us and we are His possessions;
>   we are His people, the flock He shepherds.
>
> Offer thanksgiving as you enter His gates,
>   sing hymns of praise as you approach His courts;
> give thanks to Him and bless His name,
>   for the LORD is good.

Introduction to the New Testament

The New Testament tells us about Jesus and His Church. Jesus was born as a Baby in Bethlehem and He grew up in Nazareth. When He was thirty years old, He began to travel all around Israel to preach the Good News of God's forgiveness and His desire for us to live in His love.

Jesus taught with stories and examples from everyday life. He performed miracles to show that He was God's Son. On Holy Thursday, He even gave us the gift of the Sacrament of His Body and Blood, the Eucharist.

Even though Jesus spoke about mercy and love, some people rejected Him. On Good Friday, they nailed Him to the Cross and He died for our sins. He rose from the dead three days later, on Easter Sunday, and He appeared to His Apostles.

Then, forty days later, He went up into heaven. The Father and the Son sent the Holy Spirit upon the Apostles and the Blessed Virgin Mary, so that they could share Jesus' message with the world.

Beyond the four Gospels, there is the Acts of the Apostles, which tells the story of the early days of the Church. There are also the letters of St. Paul and St. John and other Apostles, which tell us how to live like Christ in today's world.

The Annunciation

Gabriel, an Angel of God, visited a young girl named Mary at her home in Nazareth, a small town in Galilee. Mary was soon going to marry Joseph, a carpenter.

Gabriel surprised Mary when he greeted her by saying, "Hail, full of grace! The Lord is with you." His words frightened her because she did not know what they meant.

Seeing her fear, God's Angel told Mary not to be afraid because she had found favor with God. Gabriel went on to say that she was to give birth to a Son and name Him Jesus. He would rule the people forever.

Mary asked the Angel how this was going to come about. Gabriel replied that the Spirit of God would come upon her. Her Child, born of the power of God, would be called His Son.

Gabriel also told Mary that Elizabeth, her cousin, was carrying a child as well. Although Elizabeth was thought to be too old to have a child, God made it possible.

After hearing all that the Angel had to say, Mary showed her deep trust in God. She said humbly, "I am the servant of the Lord. Let it be done to me as you say." Gabriel then left Mary.

Luke 1

The Visitation

Mary was very happy that the Angel had told her all of these wonderful things, and she was also happy that her cousin, Elizabeth, was going to have a baby. But Mary realized that her cousin was quite old, and it would be very difficult for her.

She decided to leave her home and to travel to where Elizabeth lived so she could help her for a few months. Truly showing how generous she was, Mary did not think of her own problems. She simply wanted to help another.

When Mary arrived, Elizabeth greeted her and said, "Blessed are you among women, and blessed is the fruit of your womb." Elizabeth asked her why the Mother of her Lord would come to visit her.

Elizabeth already knew that Mary was going to have a Baby and that the Baby was the Son of God. How did she know this? It was because her own baby, John the Baptist, who was not even born yet, leaped in her womb to celebrate the arrival of Jesus.

Mary was now even happier, for this showed her the wonder of God's plan. She thanked and praised God in a song that begins, "My soul proclaims the greatness of the Lord and my spirit rejoices in God my Savior." *Luke 1*

The Birth of Jesus

Around that time, the Roman emperor, Augustus Caesar, wanted to know how many people were in his empire. The emperor ordered that everybody go to the town or city where they came from so they could be counted.

Joseph's and Mary's families were originally from Bethlehem, so they traveled there. This was not easy because Mary was about to have a Baby. When they arrived in Bethlehem, there were so many people that there was no room for them in the inn, so they had to stay outside in a stable where animals were kept.

During the night, Mary gave birth to a Baby Boy Whom they named Jesus. He was the Son of God and the Son of Mary. They wrapped Him up and laid Him in a manger while the animals nearby gathered around Him to help keep Him warm. *Luke 2*

The Three Wise Men

The Holy Family was poor and seemed unimportant in the world, but they received some visitors when the Baby was born.

There were shepherds staying in the fields and taking care of their sheep. An Angel visited them and announced to them that Jesus was born. They all got up and went to the stable where the Holy Family was staying so they could see Him for themselves.

Then there were three Wise Men who came from the East. They were called Magi. The Magi used to look at the stars to find out what was going to happen in the future. They saw that a Savior was born for the Jewish people and for all the people of the earth.

They set out from their homes and traveled to Bethlehem where they kneeled before Jesus and presented their gifts to Him: gold, incense, and a type of perfume. *Matthew 2; Luke 2*

The Presentation

Eight days after Jesus was born, Joseph and Mary gave Him the name that had been given to Him by the Angel Gabriel: Jesus. This name means "the Lord saves," and it tells us what Jesus came into the world to do.

Then, when Jesus was forty days old, Joseph and Mary took Him to the Temple for the Presentation.

There, they met Simeon, who had been praying to see the Savior of Israel. As soon as he saw Jesus, he knew that his prayers had been answered. He thanked God for this special gift.

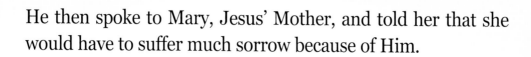

He then spoke to Mary, Jesus' Mother, and told her that she would have to suffer much sorrow because of Him.

They also met a woman named Anna who had also been in the Temple for many years. She, too, thanked and praised God for having seen Jesus.

Luke 2

Jesus Is Lost in the Temple

When Jesus was twelve, He, Joseph, and Mary went down to Jerusalem to celebrate the holy days. When it was time to go back home, Joseph and Mary traveled with different groups. They did not realize that Jesus was not with either one of them.

They quickly went back to Jerusalem and, with anxious hearts, looked for Him for three days. On the third day, they found Him in the Temple. He was speaking with the doctors of the law. The doctors were amazed that even though He was so young, He knew so much about God's ways.

When Mary asked Him why He had stayed behind in the Temple and caused such worry for her and Joseph, He answered that He had to do His Father's work. He was reminding them that God was His Father. He then went home with Joseph and Mary to Nazareth where He remained obedient to them.

Luke 2

The Baptism of Jesus

When Jesus was about thirty years old, He left home to begin His work. He was going to proclaim the Good News to the people.

One of the first things that He did was to travel to the Jordan River where His cousin, John the Baptist, encouraged people to tell their sins and ask forgiveness. He then baptized them. John was telling everyone who would listen about One Who was to come Who was mightier than he. This was the One Whom God had promised to send to free them and all people from their sins.

Jesus went up to John and asked to be baptized. At first, John did not want to baptize Jesus. He knew Who He was, and He realized that it was Jesus Who should be baptizing him and not the other way around. But Jesus said that this was the way it had to be done.

While John was baptizing Jesus, the Holy Spirit came down upon Him in the shape of a dove. A voice from the heavens proclaimed, "You are my Beloved Son; in You I am well pleased." This was the voice of God the Father.

When each one of us is baptized, we receive that same gift of the Holy Spirit and God proclaims that we are His adopted children. *Matthew 3; Mark 1; Luke 3; John 1*

Jesus Chooses the Apostles

One day, Jesus saw two fishermen working on their nets: Simon and Andrew. He called them and told them to follow Him. They left everything and began to follow Him. Jesus even gave Simon a new name. From then on, he was called Peter.

That same day he saw two other fishermen, brothers named James and John. They were working on their father's boat. Jesus also called them to follow Him, and they left what they were doing and followed Him.

He met a man named Matthew who was collecting taxes. Usually people greatly disliked tax collectors, but Jesus called him to follow Him as well.

In all, Jesus chose twelve men to follow Him as Apostles. They were to travel around with Him and learn all about God's ways. Then, when He was no longer with them, they would go out into the world to preach the Good News.

Matthew 4; Mark 1—3; Luke 5—6

The Wedding Feast of Cana

One day, Jesus went to a wedding feast with His Mother and some of His friends. They ran out of wine, and Mary went to Jesus so He would do something.

There were six stone jars there, each filled with water. Jesus blessed them and He changed the water into wine.

The servants took some of the wine to the man in charge. He tasted it and called the groom over because he was very confused. Usually, at weddings, people serve the good wine first and then later they serve a lesser wine. But the wine that the servants had brought him was better than any wine that they had served all day.

This was Jesus' first miracle. Over the next three years, He was to do many more miracles to show people that He had been sent by God.

John 2

A Great Catch of Fish

One afternoon, while Jesus was teaching the people, He noticed that a boat was nearby. The fishermen were washing their nets.

After teaching, Jesus got into the boat and told the fishermen to go out onto the Sea of Galilee. He then told them to throw their nets into the water to catch some fish. They would normally fish on the Sea of Galilee only at night, but they obeyed Jesus.

They caught so many fish that they were afraid that their boat would sink. The men called to the shore for another boat to come out and help them get all of the fish.

One of these fishermen was Peter. Jesus told him that from then on, he would go fishing after people. He was telling Peter what his new calling would mean for him.

Luke 5

Jesus Heals the Man Who Is Paralyzed

Once, Jesus was teaching inside a house. So many gathered to listen to Him that the house was full.

Four men arrived at the house, carrying their friend who could not walk. They wanted to bring him to Jesus, but they could not carry him in through the door.

So they went up on the roof, took a few of the tiles off, and lowered him down in front of Jesus so that He would heal him. He said to him, "Your sins are forgiven."

The people were surprised, because they thought that Jesus would make him walk. Some of the people there were even angry, because they said that only God can forgive sins. They did not really know Who Jesus was.

Jesus then asked the people which is easier to do, to tell the man that his sins are forgiven or to tell him to get up and walk. The obvious answer was that it was easier to heal the man's legs than to take away his sins.

Jesus then told the man to take up his mat and walk. At once, the man was healed. He got up, took his mat, and went home. The crowd was amazed by his healing and praised God. *Matthew 9; Mark 2; Luke 5*

95

The Sermon on the Mount

One day, Jesus went up on a mountain and taught the people who had gathered around Him.

He told the people that they should be humble and merciful. They should work for justice and keep God in their hearts. He told them that they should be peacemakers. He even said that those who were sad now would be blessed. He was reminding people that when they were sad or confused, they should turn to God, the Father.

Jesus also taught the people how to pray. He told them that when they pray, they should say,

"Our Father, Who art in heaven,
hallowed be Thy name;
Thy kingdom come;
Thy will be done on earth as it is in heaven.
Give us this day our daily bread;
and forgive us our trespasses,
as we forgive those who trespass against us;
and lead us not into temptation,
but deliver us from evil. Amen."

Matthew 5—7

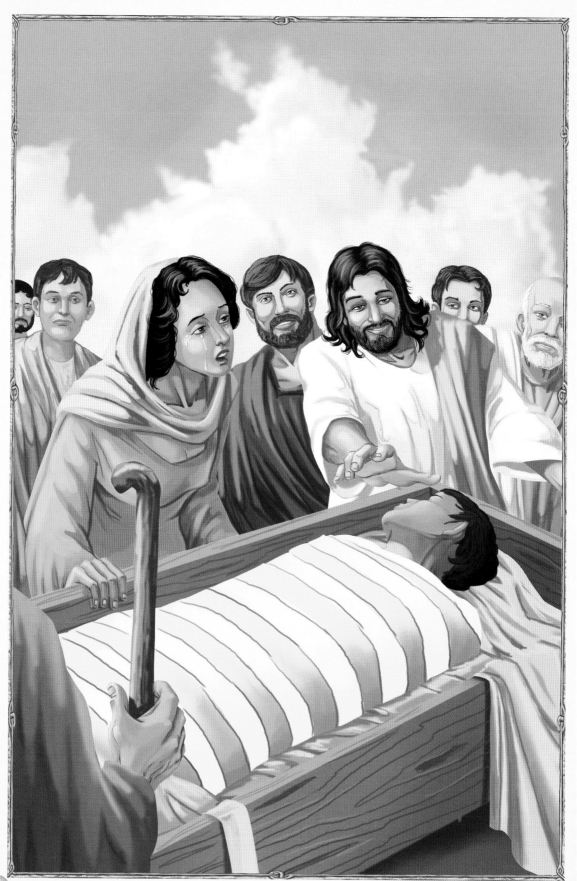

The Widow of Nain

As Jesus was traveling along, He came to a city called Nain. Just as He reached the gates of the city, He noticed that there was a funeral procession coming out.

The man who had died was young, and he was the only son of a widow. In those days, when a woman lost her husband, her children would take care of her. But now this widow did not have any children left. Jesus felt very sorry for her because she was all alone.

He told the man's mother not to cry. Jesus then went over to the men who were carrying out the young man's body, and He had them stop the procession. He then said, "Young man, I say to you, arise." At that instant, the widow's son came back to life. Jesus then gave the young man to his mother.

Everyone who heard about what Jesus did was filled with wonder. He had just brought someone back from the dead. Only God could do that. The news of what Jesus did in Nain spread to the whole region.

When Jesus worked this miracle, He was also teaching all of us. Sooner or later, everyone dies. But Jesus was promising that He will raise us all from the dead to live with Him in heaven forever.

Luke 7

The Multiplication of the Loaves and Fish

More and more people began to follow Jesus to listen to His teaching and to see His miracles.

Once, while He was with a crowd in the desert, the Apostles told Him that it was getting late, and He should tell the people that they needed to go into the town to get themselves some food. Jesus told the Apostles that they should feed the people.

The Twelve told Him that all the food they had were five loaves of bread and two fish. They then brought Jesus the loaves and the fish, and He prayed over them. He gave thanks to the Father, and then He broke the bread and fish and had the Apostles give them to the people.

Many people were there that day, over five thousand. Yet, when the Apostles gave some bread and fish to each of them, everybody had enough to eat. In fact, when they were finished eating, they gathered whatever was left over and put it into some baskets. They collected twelve baskets of food.

Matthew 14; Mark 6; Luke 9; John 6

Jesus Walks on the Water

After the people finished eating, Jesus went off alone to pray. Meanwhile, the Apostles had gotten into their boats and they were crossing the sea.

During the night, the water began to get rough and the winds grew strong. A storm was coming up and the Apostles became frightened. All of a sudden, they saw Jesus walking toward them on the water. At first they thought it was a ghost, but Jesus told them not to worry. It was He.

Jesus invited Peter to get out of the boat and walk toward Him. At first Peter got out and started to walk across the water, just

as Jesus had asked him to do. Then he realized what he was doing, and he became afraid and asked Jesus to save him. Just as Peter started to sink, Jesus grabbed him by the hand and asked him why he had not trusted in Him.

He and Peter got into the boat, and Jesus then made the winds and the sea calm. The Apostles saw that Jesus could even tell nature what to do for He truly was the Son of God.

Matthew 14; Mark 6; John 6

Jesus Preaches from the Boat

There were times that Jesus preached His message to the crowds by the sea. Sometimes He simply went from one side of the Sea of Galilee to the other by boat.

One time, though, there was a large crowd. He knew that there were too many people there to hear what He was saying, so He asked the Apostles to take Him a little way from the shore. Then, standing in the boat, He began to preach to the people.

He even used examples from the sea when He preached. People wanted to know what it would be like at the end of time. He said that it is like when a fisherman puts his net in the water. When he brings it up, some of the fish are fat and delicious, but other fish are small or ugly. The good ones he keeps, the others he throws back into the water. *Matthew 13*

The Transfiguration

Most of the time, Jesus looked like a common person. Once in a while, though, He let the Apostles see Who He really is: the Son of God.

One day, He went up a mountain with Peter, James, and John. When they reached the top, He suddenly became glowing white. The Apostles looked up and they saw Moses and Elijah standing on either side of Him.

Moses gave Israel the Law, so his being there meant that Jesus had come to fulfill the Law. Elijah was one of the prophets, so his being there meant that Jesus had come to fulfill what the prophets had said.

Confused, Peter did not even know what to say. He asked Jesus whether he should build three tents on the mountain: one for Jesus, one for Moses, and one for Elijah.

Just then, a cloud covered them. They heard a voice from the cloud saying, "This is My beloved Son, My Chosen One. Listen to Him." It was the voice of the Father.

When the Apostles looked up again, Moses and Elijah were gone. Jesus let the Apostles see Who He really was so that when He died on the Cross, they would not be afraid.

Matthew 17; Mark 9; Luke 9

Jesus and the Children

One day when Jesus was resting, some people brought a group of children for Him to bless. At first the Apostles wanted to send them away so that Jesus could rest a bit.

But when Jesus heard what was going on, He told them to bring the children right over. He blessed them and told them to be good.

When He was finished, He turned to the Apostles and told them that they should never keep the little children away. It was for the little ones that He came into the world.

It was small children who were innocent and good and kind and who showed how we should all be. In fact, Jesus told people that they could never hope to go to heaven if they did not become like little children.

What Jesus was saying is that sometimes grown-ups get too busy and they worry about too many things. They have to learn to slow down and see the beautiful things all around them like children do.

He also told people that they should be very careful of what they say and do in front of children. They should teach them only good things. *Matthew 19; Mark 10; Luke 18*

The Good Samaritan

Jesus often taught the people with stories. One day, someone asked Him whom we should love. He told the person that we should love God and we should love our neighbors. When that man asked Jesus who his neighbor was, Jesus told the story of the Good Samaritan.

There was a man who was going down from Jerusalem to Jericho. Along the way, some robbers hurt him and took everything he had. They left him wounded by the side of the road. Two men walked by the man, not stopping to help him.

Then a Samaritan came upon the man who was hurt. The Jewish people in Israel did not like Samaritans, and the Samaritans did not like the Jewish people. Still, it was the Samaritan who stopped to see how the man was. He put bandages on his wounds, and then picked him up and put him on his donkey.

The Samaritan then took the man to a nearby inn. He gave the innkeeper some money to take care of this stranger. He also told him that if it cost more than he had left, he would repay him on his way back. Even though he seemed an unlikely choice, the Samaritan turned out to be that man's neighbor.

Luke 10

Martha and Mary

Jesus' three friends, Martha, Mary, and their brother, Lazarus, lived just outside of Jerusalem. When He would go up to the Temple, He would stay at their house.

One time when He visited them, Martha had been working all day long to make sure that everything was just right for His visit. She had worked and worked until she was exhausted. Even when He arrived, she kept right on working to get the supper ready because she wanted to make sure that He enjoyed His meal.

Mary, on the other hand, did not do all that much. Once Jesus arrived, she sat down and simply listened to what He was saying. Every time that Martha entered the room and saw her sister just sitting there, she got more and more angry. Finally, she had had enough. She went up to Jesus and asked Him to tell Mary to help her.

Jesus said something that surprised her. He said that she had been so busy doing things that she had even forgotten to be nice to Him. Mary, though, had spent the whole evening with Him. Mary, and not Martha, had made the right choice.

We are just like Mary whenever we put aside what we are doing and visit with Jesus in prayer.

Luke 10

The Prodigal Son

One day, Jesus told a story about the meaning of true forgiveness.

He began by saying that there was a man who had two sons. The younger son went up to his father one day and asked for all the money he would get when his father died.

The father collected the money and gave it to his son. The son traveled far away and wasted the money on all kinds of silly things. Eventually, he did not have even a penny to his name.

To make some money, he got a job feeding pigs. He longed to be given the food that he was giving to the pigs, but no one offered him anything. He soon realized that even the servants at his father's house had more than enough to eat, so he decided to return home.

While he was still a little way from home, his father saw him in the distance and ran up to him. He hugged him and told him that he forgave him.

The older brother was upset because his father had forgiven his selfish brother. But the father told the older brother that he had to celebrate, because his younger son had been as good as dead, and now he was alive again.

Luke 15

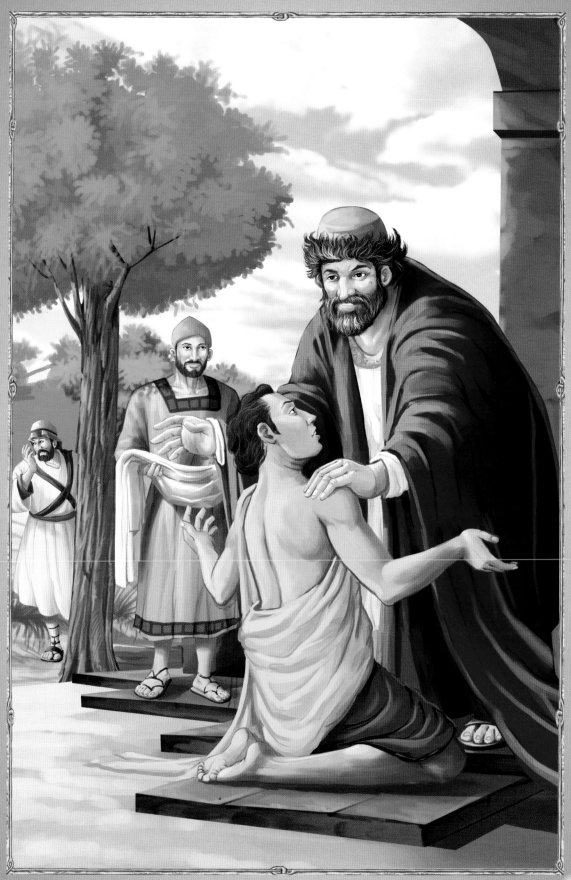

Jesus Raises Lazarus

*O*nce, while Jesus was away on a trip, He got word that His friend Lazarus, the brother of Martha and Mary, was very sick. He did not go to see him right away, though, because Jesus knew that God was going to use this turn of events for something very important.

After two days, Jesus told the disciples that it was time to visit Lazarus. He told them that Lazarus had died but that all would be well. By the time they got to Lazarus's village, he already had been dead for four days.

Martha and Mary each went out to talk with Jesus. They were upset that their brother had died, but they also trusted that Jesus could do miracles.

Jesus wept as He went to the tomb where they had placed His friend. He then ordered that the large rock in front of the tomb be moved.

After praying to His Father, Jesus said, "Lazarus, come out!" Lazarus came back to life and out of the tomb. Jesus told the people standing there to help Lazarus get out of his burial clothes.

Many people who saw what Jesus had done or who even heard about it began to believe that Jesus was God's Son.

John 11

Jesus Enters Jerusalem

About a week later, Jesus decided that it was time to let all of the people know Who He was.

He told His disciples to get a small donkey for Him to ride into Jerusalem. One of the prophets had said that the Messiah would come into Jerusalem just this way. Now all of the people could see that Jesus was the Messiah.

As He went along, the people cut off branches from the trees, and they laid them and flowers and robes along His way. They were showing Jesus signs of great honor, for many of them had seen His miraculous deeds.

They also cried out, "Hosanna! Blessed is He who comes in the name of the Lord!" They were greeting the Messiah, the One Who would free them from all of their enemies. They were so filled with joy and excitement that they shouted louder and louder.

The leaders of Jerusalem told Jesus that He should try to get the people to quiet down. They were afraid that there would be a riot. But Jesus refused to do as they had asked of Him. He told them that even if He were to tell them to be quiet, then the stones in the buildings would begin to cry out instead. *Matthew 21; Mark 11; Luke 19; John 12*

The Last Supper

The next Thursday evening, Jesus sat down to a special supper with His Apostles. They were eating the Passover meal to celebrate the day that God freed the Jewish people from slavery in Egypt.

While they were eating, Jesus took bread in His hands. He blessed it, broke it, and, while giving it to the Apostles for them to eat, said, "This is My Body, which will be given up for you."

He then took a cup of wine in His hands. After giving thanks, He gave it to the Apostles to drink and said, "This is the chalice of My Blood of the new and eternal covenant. It will be poured out for you and for many for the forgiveness of sins."

After giving the Apostles the bread and the cup, He said, "Do this in memory of Me." This was the first time that Jesus celebrated Mass. He was giving the Apostles and us the gift of the Eucharist, the very gift of Himself. *Matthew 26; Mark 14; Luke 22*

The Agony in the Garden

After the meal was over, Jesus took His disciples out to a garden that was located on the other side of the city. He asked them to sit while He prayed. Jesus moved apart from them and took Peter, James, and John with Him.

There, in the garden, Jesus left these three Apostles by themselves to keep watch while He went on a little further into the garden. He began to pray to the Father. Jesus wanted to do the Father's Will, but He also was afraid.

Jesus knew that the Father was asking Him to die on the Cross for us. He said to the Father that if there was any other way it could be done, then let it be done that way. But if not, He said, "Your Will be done!"

Three times Jesus broke away from His prayers and went to see how the Apostles were doing. He had asked them to keep watch with Him, but each time they had fallen asleep.

Finally, by the third time, they heard the soldiers arriving with Judas. Judas had come into the garden to hand Jesus over to the authorities. He went up to Jesus and kissed Him. The soldiers then grabbed Jesus and took Him away. Even though Jesus could have stopped them, He did not resist, for He knew that this was the Father's Will.

Matthew 26; Mark 14; Luke 22

"Behold the Man"

The soldiers first took Jesus to the High Priest to question Him. They wanted to find something to charge Him with so that they could put Him to death. The best that they could do was to get some witnesses to say some untrue things about Him, but their stories did not match.

Next, they took Jesus to the Roman governor, Pilate. They did this because they did not have the authority to put anyone to death. They wanted Pilate to do this.

But Pilate was confused. The more he talked with Jesus, the more he realized that Jesus had not done anything that deserved putting Him to death. He wanted to free Jesus and even offered to release either Him or another man who was a murderer. The crowd shouted out that they wanted the murderer set free and not Jesus.

Pilate then had Jesus beaten. The soldiers whipped Him and put a crown of thorns on His head. Pilate was hoping that when the crowd saw how bad He looked, they would feel sorry for Him and let Him be set free.

When he brought Jesus out he said, "Behold the Man!" But the crowd only shouted all the louder that He had to be put to death. So Pilate ordered that He must die upon the Cross.

John 18—19

Jesus Carries His Cross

So they set out to take Jesus, who was carrying His Cross, to the place where He was to die.

Along the way, He met His Mother. There was so much pain in her eyes, for she saw and felt the pain of her beloved Son.

He also met a group of women from Jerusalem who were crying. He told them not to cry for Him, but for themselves and for their children. Jesus said this because He knew that the people of Jerusalem would suffer much in the next years.

Along the way, the soldiers forced a man named Simon, who was passing by, to help Jesus carry the Cross to the location where He would die. *Matthew 27; Mark 15; Luke 23; John 19*

127

Jesus Dies on the Cross

When they reached the place where Jesus was to die, the soldiers nailed Him to the Cross. They then took His clothes and divided them among themselves. This happened around noon on Friday.

For the next three hours, Jesus hung upon the Cross. Even then, though, He was not

thinking about Himself. Jesus was worried about everyone else. He asked God the Father to forgive the people who had nailed Him to the Cross. Jesus spoke with one of the thieves who was on a cross alongside of Him. The thief expressed his belief in Jesus, and He promised him that he would be in heaven that very day.

Then, at three in the afternoon, Jesus gave up His Spirit and He died. They buried Him in a tomb that was not too far away.

Matthew 27; Mark 15; Luke 23; John 19

Jesus Rises from the Dead

On Sunday morning, some of the women who had followed Jesus decided to go out to the tomb to anoint His Body. There had been no time to do this on Friday. Along the way, they were wondering who would help them roll back the big stone that closed off the tomb. But when they got there, they found that the stone had already been rolled back.

There was an Angel in the tomb who announced that God had raised Jesus from the dead. Even though they were afraid because of the Angel's news, they ran to tell the disciples all that they had seen and heard.

At first, the disciples wondered if what they were saying could be true. But then Jesus appeared to them. They saw that He was alive again, and they were filled with joy. They cried out songs of praise, saying especially, "Alleluia!"—a word that means, "May the Lord be praised!"

Matthew 28; Mark 16; Luke 24; John 20

The Road to Emmaus

That same day, two disciples were walking along from Jerusalem to a town named Emmaus. They had not yet heard that Jesus had risen from the dead.

Along the way, they met a stranger. It was Jesus, but they did not know this yet. The stranger asked them why they were so sad. They explained that they had followed Jesus for a long time and thought that He was the Promised One of God, but that He had died on Friday.

Jesus then explained to them that all of this had to happen. He spoke about how the Law and the prophets had foretold the events of the last few days.

They decided to stop for the night at an inn. The disciples invited the stranger to stay with them. As they sat down for their evening meal, the stranger blessed the bread, broke it, and gave it to them. At once, they recognized Jesus. As soon as they realized Who He was, He disappeared.

The two men immediately got up and began the return journey to Jerusalem to speak with other of Jesus' disciples. These disciples were eager to tell the men that Jesus had risen. For their part, the two men told about meeting a stranger and then recognizing Jesus when He broke the bread.

Luke 24

Doubting Thomas

That same evening, the disciples were all gathered together where they had eaten the Last Supper. They had locked the doors because they were afraid.

Having risen from the dead, Jesus was able to come right through the locked doors. He said to the disciples, "Peace be with you." He then breathed on the disciples—in much the same way as God had done when He created the first person, Adam, by breathing on him. It was like the disciples had a new beginning.

There was one disciple who was not present that night. His name was Thomas. He said that he would not believe that Jesus had risen from the dead until he could touch the wounds to His side and His hands that Jesus had suffered on the Cross.

A week later, the disciples were gathered together again, but this time Thomas was with them. Jesus appeared again and told Thomas that he could touch the wounds in His hands, feet, and side if he wanted to.

Thomas now knew that Jesus had truly risen. He fell on his knees and all he could say was, "My Lord and my God!" Even though he had doubted, Jesus gave Thomas a chance to believe in Him.

John 20

Peter, the Shepherd of the Church

Another time the disciples went out fishing at night, as was their custom. In the morning, Jesus appeared to them on the shore and called out to ask them if they had caught anything. They said that they had not, and Jesus told them to try the other side of the boat. They threw in their nets and caught more fish than they had ever caught before.

When they arrived on the shore, Jesus had prepared some breakfast for them. When they had finished eating, Jesus asked Peter, "Do you love Me?" Peter said, "Yes," and Jesus told him, "Feed my lambs." Jesus asked Peter a second time, "Do you love Me?" Peter said, "Yes," and Jesus told him, "Take care of my sheep."

Finally, Jesus asked Peter a third time, "Do you love Me?" Peter realized that Jesus was reminding him that he had denied Him three times. So Peter said, "Yes, Lord." Jesus said, "Feed my sheep."

Jesus is the Good Shepherd. Since He was returning to heaven, He was giving Peter the job of being the shepherd of His sheep. In other words, Jesus was making Peter the first Pope. Peter was to follow Jesus.

John 21

Jesus Ascends to Heaven

Jesus appeared to the disciples over the next several weeks, and He also appeared to a number of other people. There was one time that He appeared to over five hundred people, all at the same time.

Jesus stayed with His disciples for forty days, and He taught them all about the faith. At the end of the forty days, it was time for Jesus to go to be with the Father.

So Jesus led the disciples out of Jerusalem to a hill called the Mount of Olives. While they were watching, He went up into the clouds and disappeared from their sight. The disciples were very confused, for they wanted Him to stay. But it was time for them to begin their new job of preaching the Good News to all the nations upon the earth.

While the disciples were still looking up into the skies, they saw two Angels who asked them what they were doing. They said, "Why are you looking for Jesus who has gone up into the heavens? He will return as you have seen Him leave."

The disciples went back to Jerusalem, and they entered the room where they had eaten the Last Supper. There they and the Blessed Virgin Mary waited and prayed for the Spirit Whom Jesus had promised to them. *Acts 1*

The Coming of the Holy Spirit

Ten days after Jesus had gone up into the heavens, the Apostles and Mary were gathered together again to pray. All of a sudden they heard a great wind. They looked around and saw flames of fire over each of them. This was the gift of the Holy

Spirit. Jesus had not left them alone. He and God the Father had sent them the Holy Spirit to teach them and guide them as they preached the Good News.

Peter went out on the porch of the place where they were staying. He spoke to the people in his own language, but everyone in the crowd could hear his words as if he were speaking in their own languages. This was a great miracle, for there were people in the crowd from all over the world. The Holy Spirit gave all the Apostles this gift so that they would understand how much God loves them.

Acts 2

141